A Shade Pulled Just Barely

poems by

Anne Bucey

Finishing Line Press
Georgetown, Kentucky

A Shade Pulled Just Barely

Poems

ACKNOWLEDGMENTS

Tiger's Eye: A Journal of Poetry: "Sabbath"
The Rose in the World: "Lightning Bugs," "There's nothing wrong with sadness"
The Healing Muse: "Before the Diagnosis"
Tipton Poetry Journal: "Midlife Crisis"

Publisher: Leah Huete de Maines
Editor: Christen Kincaid
Cover Art: Karen Klecka Weyandt
Author Photo: David Bucey
Cover Design: Elizabeth Maines McCleavy

Order online: www.finishinglinepress.com
also available on amazon.com

Author inquiries and mail orders:
Finishing Line Press
PO Box 1626
Georgetown, Kentucky 40324
USA

Contents

Sabbath 1

Pink 2

Housecoats 3

When I had help 4

Mother Rage 5

If Only You 6

What I Don't Say Because He Is There............................ 7

Daughter 8

Fresh 9

Summer Reception.. 10

Yellow Fruit 11

Midlife Crisis... 12

Hard and Soft 15

Oatmeal Love 16

The Masseur 17

Your White Tux Shirt 18

Excess 19

Lightning Bugs.. 20

There's nothing wrong with sadness 21

Before the Diagnosis 22

Annie 23

for Dave

Sabbath

First, you drink half
a glass of wine
on the porch.

The lightning bugs
are low to the ground and few
and you are alone
with the dog and the heavy,
moist trees, their deep
pockets of green and the eyes
of the sky gathered in the branches
before the summer night
shuts them. The wine is cold
and delicate and you can almost
forget the rusty keen of the front loader
lumbering in the neighbors' yard
(what could drive a man
to dig trenches on a Friday night?)
But the scent of gardenia
brings you back
to the porch and the dog
and the fading light.
Everything that's white—
the lace collars of daisies,
the phlox, the snow hydrangeas—
grows whiter by the minute,
as dusk extends a velvet arm,
holding fortitude,
the clarity of white,
in a dark embrace.

And then you go back inside
to the yellow walls of the kitchen,
where you reheat
the dinner plate.

Pink

the color of my blouse
           the color of
this hospital gown,
which feels surprisingly warm,
the texture of a newborn's
nap, so that I thank the young
lady who gives it
to me before I undress, before
she arranges the right frontal lobe
of my chest on a smooth
metal platform, lifted
for support. Oh, what they do
to make the pain
more bearable—wrapping my body
in the color of a girl, like this
nurse's assistant,
who anchors, secures, then,
from the distance
of instrument control,
whispers instructions:
        don't move, don't breathe
so that I do
hold my breath, submit
to stillness, a powder blue
powerlessness, till I hear
her small voice,
hushed and invisible,
say, *OK, it's OK,*
        you can breathe now,

        you can breathe
        again.

Housecoats

She is wild about my house
which has such potential,
I mean you could do
so much with it, if you
weren't me but this
designer. And I am following the cut
of her black jacket,
which is perfectly correct,
just grazing the hip,
while her scarf seems to whisper
the most interesting
secrets in shades that highlight
the color of her red brown
hair and tortoise shell frames,
which sweep the full scale
of the room, surveying its
appearance, sadly noticing the flaws
in the countertop, shining
like pimples on a very
young man. Like me,
I say in my khaki capris.
Like my ceramic dove
and the clever way the family
pictures are arranged.
But I wonder
if she were to remove
her glasses and her shoes
and sit down for a while,
whether she could hear my house talk,
the way it does when we,
the house and I,
are alone reminiscing,
when we are two grey-headed
ladies in our housecoats
late at night.

When I had help

she waited at the bus stop
tall, big boned, asking
after the children, who
she meant to raise
one day a week.
In the house she put me
in my place. Said,
Go on upstairs now and
lie down so you stay pretty
like your mother.

Mother Rage

A thin reed of passion
trembling with anger
hovers over her brazen
body ready to strike.
Like a snake coiled and
hissing, I hold myself erect,
hoping that my eyes alone—
gold and spitting like
fresh fire in the grate—
might singe the shell of her
ego enough to let me in.
My hand slaps the air
instead of her face, though
I can see her flinch
as if we both expected
different. It is all I can do
to make myself just
scare her, which scares
me too. What window
can I shatter to make our blood
run together again? Her eyes,
like glass, reflect me
back to myself, while she
huddles in an armchair,
waiting out the storm.

If Only You

It was a slip
of the tongue, yours,

but the wound blossomed
like a rose
outside the back
door of my heart, knocking,
so, I let it in.

Then it grew—
a pink amoeba under the microscope
of my thinking.

I handed you a hunk
of black salve and schooled you
to touch it gently,
pat it lightly
with your own heart's
finger.

You looked at me, blue
fear in your eyes.
And you tried.

But in your voice
I could hear,
I am not handy.

What I Don't Say Because He Is There

If I lost him,
I would write a poem
painting his eyes
water color blue, circling
the softer side of his
face when it turns
to cold melons
in December, blushed
and sweeter than he
will ever know.

If he were gone,
I would sing
the blues in the way
we loved,
the way I might
have never known him
fully, a man dogged
by a borrower
and lender's code
of conduct,
hard and unflinching.

And I might never hold
or smell his
grace until his absence
resurrects the love
we shaped like
clay in the dark—
a gray smoke fired
bird, its voice
animated by ours,
cooing.

Daughter

When she fell in love,
I fell too
into the silvery cloud
of her happiness
where I floated
and allowed myself to rest
for an afternoon,
giving in to the letting go of her
like the dead
who watch their own sleeping
bodies from the far corner
of a room.

And I could see it—
this thin film of beauty, like an aura, following
her darkened shape
as she walked down the hall
and disappeared behind a door,
where the first rush of heat
burst from the shower—the sound
of which did nothing to mute
the sound of the beauty, small
and clear like the ring
of crystal in a glass, still
hanging in the air
where she'd stood
before me.

What
holds it up
but the buoyant
thrill of
falling?

Fresh
for Dan (1956-1990)

Now that you have been dead
for so many years,
I would like to bury you myself—
dig a hole, make it sweet
with mulch and lime
cover you with cool, naked dirt,
pressed down, smoothed
with my own two hands. I would
not carve your name in stone—no
but there would be a valentine
on the mound,
growing from your buried heart,
edges trimmed in gold lace,
the cut-out, corseted figure of a woman
standing in the center of it,
smiling at the foolishness
of love. Your poems
in manual type would peek
from the ground like shy
violets, a cluster of daffodils
would recall the sunny days
of our freshman year
and a French horn
would cry loud and slightly out
of tune, from some place you
had played with thrill
and abandon.

I would sing over all these things.

And what I never said of love
would soak you
like fresh rain.

Summer Reception

Every big white oak,
leaning into my porch,
is a gentleman caller,
bearing armloads
of leaves heavy
with sweat.
You can hardly see the sky
for the green
of their eagerness to talk
to me in giant silences,
to stand in my
presence like tall and
reverent men waiting
for an invitation
and for the sound
of the first crickets—
a little night music
with which to serenade
a lady.
I close my eyes, rock
and slip slowly
into the dance.

Yellow Fruit

As a girl,
those girls who knew
were a mystery to me—
big golden worlds
that billowed gently
over dormitory lawns
on Friday afternoons
in the spring. They would
undress openly
in the girls' bathroom
and walk to the shower,
letting us look if we cared.

Now that I know,
I can feel the curves of this luminous orb
swelling in me and I want
to try again, to live again
those afternoons of sunlight
lying on the lawn. I am inclined
to take off my winter coat
and let my legs walk a man
into oblivion.

Midlife Crisis

One day she woke
up and saw she
was a grape, too ripe
to be succulent, almost
too ripe to taste,
hanging from a vine
that wrapped aging
fingers around the
stainless in her
kitchen.

So, she put on
a skirt with pleats
that rode wildly
away from the sensible
caps of her knees
and went to Target
listening for
a whistle. It
could have come
from the short, ruddy
guy outside, waiting
for the bus or
his buddy, for that matter,
because it really
didn't—only that her calves
could command
such a quick,
lusty glance from
a perfect
stranger.

Later, when the priest
kissed her
in the deserted coat
room, not once
but twice
and her legs lit up
like flashing sirens,
she emerged from the dream
with the sobering
thought that she'd been
picked before, seasons
ago, picked small
and green.

Then she rose in
the night to
comfort the terror
of the brittle vine, of the passing
of many nights, knowing
the late hour's
ghostly visitation
was surrounded
by the days and years
of loving a man
and the children they
bore, who, in turn, bore
them up, like Handel's
full chorus—
announcing the passion,
pleading
for redemption.

The boy of eight
years looked up
from his pillow
and said how he wished
he'd savored the bliss
of kindergarten—*savored*
he said! And his mother
shook her head and
wondered where
he'd heard that
word—how
did he
know?

Hard and Soft

There are hard and soft
parts of ourselves,
the shell and the meat,
the wing and the beak.
There is the back turned,
its long vertical line refusing
and the skin
that gives a little
with touch.
Even the heart is hard
and soft, its muscles taut
and shining, its fist
buried in the soft tissue
of the animal body,
opening, closing,
the thin membrane
of its contours,
its secret, brittle
calcium, warm
with life.

Oatmeal Love

Some days, all I want
is to make Grandmother's
oatmeal cookies, not fretting
over why my love cracks
and splits the way she split spring
bulbs, cloves pulling away,
sending down vagrant roots
into the darkness of
the garden bed.
Just let me follow the old
recipe, watch raisins
bubble up in dough, stir
it only till it drops in soft, ragged
pods on tired sheets
of aluminum. If I could,
I would make them
again and again, till my legs ache
with standing at the countertop,
till my love is poured out so completely
in racks of oatmeal confections,
that I have nothing left
to give, but a love
so pure and simple,
it can be taken—
swallowed
whole.

The Masseur

In the beginning
there was Amos
in a darkened room
And Amos said
Let there be a bare woman
face down shrouded
in white

And let there be
the hills and valleys of her
back that lie still as a landscape
painting and sigh
when the weight of my hands
fall on them

And Amos gave his fingers
eyes that see and speech
that named
the countries of her flesh
and set them sailing
into the wind with
banners flying
on a wide and open
sea

And it was seven
days or seven
minutes when Amos
pulled the woman's arms
into a hymn of praise—
his warm
brown voice
singing

rest now
it is good.

Your White Tux Shirt

If your life were hidden
in a button,
it would be the one
on your white tux shirt
closest to the neck,
the one I am wiggling
through a tiny starched opening,
pulling you forward
into better light.
Old enough
to choose a flower for a girl's
gown, but you want help with this,
so I am pulling the two ends
of the collar to meet halfway
between the square of
your shoulders, all of you
gathered in a single piece—
the afternoon sun
going quickly,
the one white jewel
still centered
in my hands.

Excess

Not embarrassing really. Just strange, fabulous
and a little disturbing. They burst in the room, arms

pumping, legs marching, pink faces ablaze
with the brazenness of the game.

We want excess, we want excess! Two little girls—
no more than 4 and 6,

younger maybe—raising the roof with a single file chant,
calling on all the you-go-girl powers

that rain on children, unschooled in the difference
between too much and enough. Girl bodies

in the buff, not a stitch on but wearing the purest delight
in the abandonment of clothes

and quiet voices. I watched them march, my moral voice
quieted, the one that inside

asked who taught them that word, a word spilling over
and over, like water from the rim of a pot,

like puppies let loose from a day in a pen. Who taught them
to sing it, demand it, wave it like a flag? As I write

in this second home garage apartment,
as I count the flowers of pleasure, measure

restraint with a teaspoon of control, I push harder
at the question of where they learned it—the game, its music—

and of how the ocean breaks and washes lavishly—
before coming to itself and spilling again

Lightning Bugs

I see stars in the trees
        maybe hundreds—
    flotsam of light
on the warm currents
        of a summer night—kin
   less to lightening
than fish
     in a dark aquarium—
aimless,
       drifting,
              careless,
it seems,
    that as the dark deepens,

      they rise.

There's nothing wrong with sadness

I can lean against her long black hair
and smell its thick abundance.
She is my companion,
my mother.
There is no one else I have to please.
I can ride her like a horse
and trust that she will take me
where I need to go.
She does not run too fast,
she is steady; she is a fish,
resting deep in the lake—
my bottom dwelling heart.

Before the Diagnosis

I walk all the way back to where it was just
depression, then back before that to where it was

willfulness or the question of who was in charge,
to the rose room, the candle in the basement,

to the truth told slant on brick walls, to the girls
she knew, who once were her friends, to the pictures

I still have of them. And I say, let me be mother again,
do things differently, take back what I said

about the other friend, wars fought over unwashed pans,
things said to her father and to myself, less loved,

it seems, than now. Which is what I really want to bring
to the old living room; a heart not needing it to be better

than what it was with its clutter and banter and serial drama—
me and the kind mother of myself, taking it all

into one reckless hug, slaking its thirst for no resolution—
the pain, just as it was— a face in the mirror of love.

Annie

She comes to me
willingly, with slow steps
like she knows I need her: mongrel queen,
all spine and leg bone, thin
tendon, loose when she moves.
She pulls away
from my gloved hands grasping. Turns
and stares out onto
the lower creek gulch. Hears
her Maker, maybe. Or the trees,
the wind in them. Whatever she hears—
her hearing mostly gone—
is silent to my ears. Her man,
passed, her home, now his neighbor's.
Even as a young dog,
she never craved petting
and she never really belonged to him.

Anne Bucey lives part time in Virginia and part time in the mountains of Western North Carolina. She earned an undergraduate degree in history from Kenyon College, an MEd from Georgia State University and an MFA in Writing from the Naslund-Mann School of Writing at Spalding University. Certified in Spiritual Direction, she has companioned people receiving inpatient hospice care in a downtown Atlanta medical center. She has facilitated workshops for the Georgia Poetry Society's Poetry in Schools program and founded Open Mic Poetry at The Red Shoes, a center for personal and spiritual growth in Baton Rouge, Louisiana. Anne's poetry and essays have appeared in various regional and national journals, including *Arkansas Review* and *Broad River Review*, where her poem, "Canebrake," was a finalist for the 2023 Ron Rash Award.

www.ingramcontent.com/pod-product-compliance
Lightning Source LLC
Chambersburg PA
CBHW022101080426
42734CB00009B/1443